To: Mabely

From: Virginia

Beacon of Light

A JOURNEY OF HOPE
AND DISCOVERY

Compiled by Lois L. Kaufman

 PETER PAUPER PRESS, INC.
WHITE PLAINS, NEW YORK

Lighthouse locations and photo credits
appear on pages 80-81.

Designed by Taryn Sefecka

Copyright © 2003
Peter Pauper Press, Inc.
202 Mamaroneck Avenue
White Plains, NY 10601
All rights reserved
ISBN 0-88088-189-5
Printed in China
7 6 5 4 3 2 1

Visit us at www.peterpauper.com

Beacon of Light

A Journey of Hope and Discovery

INTRODUCTION

When the storm is at its height
and the night at its darkest,
the lighthouse beams its light
and guides sailors on their way.
And through life's fiercest
storms, the lights of faith,
hope, and love burn brilliantly,
helping us find our way.

L. L. K.

Keep your face
to the sunshine and
you cannot see
the shadow.

Helen Keller

Out of each experience
enough light is generated
to illuminate another
little stretch. Who knows
where it will lead?
And who can
tell where it started?

Cesar Chavez

I have often thought that the people who built lighthouses, and those who kept them, were optimists. A lighthouse is a beacon to all on the sea— a sure sign that land is near and that someone aloft is keeping a steadfast eye for their safe passage.

Fletcher Cairns

When we walk to the
edge of all the light we have
and take the step into the
darkness of the unknown,
we must believe that one of
two things must happen:
there will be something solid
for us to stand on, or we
will be taught to fly.

Patrick Overton

Life is no brief candle
to me. It is a sort of splendid
torch which I have got
a hold of for the moment,
and I want to make it burn
as brightly as possible
before handing it on to
future generations.

George Bernard Shaw

The man who has seen
the rising moon break out
of the clouds at midnight
has been present like an
archangel at the creation of
light and of the world.

Ralph Waldo Emerson

There are two ways
of spreading light:
to be the candle or the
mirror that reflects it.

Edith Wharton

Hope is like the sun,
which, as we journey
toward it, casts the
shadow of our
burden behind us.

Samuel Smiles

We don't know
who we are until we
see what we can do.

Martha Grimes

People are like stained
glass windows. They sparkle
and shine when the sun
is out, but when the darkness
sets in, their true beauty
is revealed only if there is
a light from within.

Elizabeth Kübler-Ross

There are some things
you learn best in calm,
and some in storm.

Willa Cather

In the right light, at the right time, everything is extraordinary.

Aaron Rose

Ideals are like stars;
you will not succeed in
touching them with your
hands. But like the seafaring
man on the desert of waters,
you choose them as your
guides, and following them
you will reach your destiny.

Carl Schurz

Even from a dark night
songs of beauty can be born.

Maryanne Radmacher-Hershey

Most of the important things in the world have been accomplished by people who have kept on trying when there seemed to be no hope at all.

Dale Carnegie

You must live in the present,
launch yourself on every
wave, find your eternity in
each moment. Fools stand
on their island opportunities
and look toward another land.
There is no other land,
there is no other life but this.

Henry David Thoreau

And yet, when I look up
to the sky, I somehow feel
that everything will change
for the better, that this
cruelty too shall end, that
peace and tranquility will
return once more.

Anne Frank

Be thou the rainbow
in the storms of life.
The evening beam that
smiles the clouds away,
and tints tomorrow
with prophetic ray.

Lord Byron

When it is dark enough,
you can see the stars.

Charles A. Beard

Help your brother's
boat across, and before
you know it, your own
has reached the shore.

Hindu Proverb

Hope is a waking dream.

Aristotle

Where there is hope
there is life, where there
is life there is possibility and
where there is possibility
change can occur.

Jesse Jackson

Many candles can be
kindled from one candle
without diminishing it.

Talmud

Thou didst bear unmoved
Blasts of adversity and
frosts of fate!
But the first ray of sunshine
that falls on thee
Melts thee to tears.

Henry Wadsworth Longfellow

Hope is the
pillar of the world.

African Proverb

Miracles happen
to those who
believe in them.

Bernard Berenson

Grace strikes us when
we are in great pain and
restlessness. . . . Sometimes
at that moment a wave
of light breaks into our
darkness, and it is as though
a voice were saying:
"You are accepted."

Paul Tillich

If winter comes,
can spring be far behind?

Percy Bysshe Shelley

Aim at Heaven and
you will get Earth
thrown in. Aim at Earth
and you get neither.

C. S. Lewis

I try to avoid
looking forward or
backward, and try
to keep looking upward.

Charlotte Brontë

If you hear a voice
within you say
"you cannot paint,"
then by all means paint,
and that voice will
be silenced.

Vincent van Gogh

I can see in the midst
of death, life persists,
in the midst of
untruth, truth persists,
in the midst of
darkness light persists.

Mohandas K. Gandhi

Your old men shall
dream dreams, your young
men shall see visions.

Joel 2:28 KJV

When nothing is sure,
everything is possible.

Margaret Drabble

If you can dream it,
you can do it.

Walt Disney

A rock pile ceases
to be a rock pile the
moment a single man
contemplates it,
bearing within him the
image of a cathedral.

Antoine de Saint-Exupéry

All which happens
through the
whole world happens
through hope.

Martin Luther

We stand in life
at midnight;
we are always on the
threshold of a new dawn.

Martin Luther King, Jr.

The human body
experiences a powerful
gravitational pull
in the direction of hope.
That is why the patient's
hopes are the physician's
secret weapon. They are the
hidden ingredients in
any prescription.

Norman Cousins

We have always held
to the hope, the belief,
the conviction that there is a
better life, a better world,
beyond the horizon.

Franklin D. Roosevelt

And God said,
Let there be light:
and there was light.

Genesis 1:3 KJV

No pessimist ever discovered
the secret of the stars,
or sailed to an uncharted land,
or opened a new doorway
for the human spirit.

Helen Keller

There was never a night
or a problem that could
defeat sunrise or hope.

Bern Williams

Behold, we know
not anything;
I can but trust that
good shall fall
At last—far off—
at last, to all,
And every winter
change to spring.

Alfred, Lord Tennyson

You see things; and
you say "Why?"
But I dream things
that never were;
and I say "Why not?"

George Bernard Shaw

To hope and dream is
not to ignore the practical.
It is to dress it in
colors and rainbows.

Anne Wilson Schaef

Nothing that is
beautiful is easy, but
everything is possible.

Mercedes de Acosta

As far as we can discern,
the sole purpose of
human existence is
to kindle a light in the
darkness of mere being.

Carl Gustav Jung

Hope is itself a species of
happiness, and, perhaps,
the chief happiness which
this world affords.

Samuel Johnson

Never give up, for that is
just the place and time that
the tide will turn.

Harriet Beecher Stowe

Yes, I am a dreamer.
For a dreamer is one who
can only find his way
by moonlight, and his
punishment is that he sees
the dawn before the rest
of the world.

Oscar Wilde

"For I know the plans
I have for you," declares
the LORD, "plans to prosper
you and not to harm you,
plans to give you hope
and a future."

Jeremiah 29:11 NIV

Throw your dreams
into space like a kite, and
you do not know what it
will bring back, a new life,
a new friend, a new love,
a new country.

Anaïs Nin

A little light
dispels much darkness.

Issachar Eilenburg

Stand in the light when
you want to speak out.

Crow Proverb

Faith, like light, should
always be simple and
unbending; while love,
like warmth, should
beam forth on every side,
and bend to every necessity
of our brethren.

Martin Luther

Hope is the thing
with feathers
That perches in the soul,
And sings the tune
without the words,
And never stops at all ...

Emily Dickinson

A rising tide lifts all boats.

John F. Kennedy

Stars may be seen from
the bottom of a deep well,
when they cannot be
seen from the top of the
mountain. So many things
are learned in adversity
which the prosperous man
dreams not of.

Charles Hadden Spurgeon

There are three things
I was born with in this
world, and there are three
things I will have until
the day I die: hope,
determination, and song.

Miriam Makeba

Let your hook be
always cast; in the pool
where you least expect
it will be a fish.

Ovid

Hope springs eternal
in the human breast:
Man never is, but
always to be blest.

Alexander Pope

The grand essentials to
happiness in this life are
something to do, something
to love, and something
to hope for.

Joseph Addison

All human wisdom is
summed up in two words,
—wait and hope.

Alexandre Dumas père

See everything.
Overlook a great deal.
Improve a little.

Pope John XXIII

Angels are like
lighthouses for those
passing by in storms.

Karen Goldman

Looking back, may I
be filled with gratitude;
Looking forward,
may I be filled with hope;
Looking upward,
may I be aware of strength;
Looking inward,
may I find peace.

Author unknown

The Lighthouses

Photo Credits